COGNITIVE POWER

KNOW THE ULTIMATE TRUTH OF POWER

JYOTSANA MAHOR

Made with ♥ on the Notion Press Platform
www.notionpress.com

Dedicate to

My Parents and God

Contents

Preface

Cognitive power portrays bto the mental facuilties that enable humans to process information, solve problems, make decisions and adapt to changing environments. It encompasses a range of cognitive abilities, including attention, memory, perception, reasoning and language. These cognitive functions work together to help individuals navigate the world around them, intreact with others and develop new knowledge. Coognitive power is often linked to intelligence but it extends beyond traditional IQ measures. It involves the brain's capacity to understand complex and aplly knowlegde creatively. Moreover, cognitive power is dynamic - it can be nurtured and developed through education, experience and the exercise of mental skills.

In recent years, the concept of cognitive power has gained attention in various fields such as neuro science, psychology, artificial intelligence, and education. As technology continues to evolve, the intersection between human cognitive abilities and machine intelligence raises intriguing question and the boundaries of human potential. This exploration of cognitive power invites deeper reflection on how we think, learn and grow highlighting the importance of maintaining and improving our cognitive abilities in an increasing complex and fast paced world.

Cognitive power in politics refers to the ability of individuals, groups or leaders to shape, influence and manage public opinion, political discourse and decision making processes through the strategic use of information, perception and reasonong. It involves not only the cognitive abilities of political leaders but also the ways in which citizens process, interpret and respond to political messages. in Politics, cognitive power is a critical tool for shaping narratives, framing debates and mobilizing support. Leaders, political parties and institutions often use cognitive strategies to influence how issues are understood bt the public and to guide political behaviour. This can involve the manipulation oof information, persassion through media, and the framing of political issues in ways that reasonate with the public values, emotuions and cognitive biases.

Eventual truth power is making ourselves aware of power in realistic manner. Cognitive Power enhance the capability to take decisions, helpful in understanding the responsibility towards the community. Nuclus of the book is to comprehend the power in political & administrative arena, simunteously, we indulge in transferming ourselves must bring relective change in human behaviour then only fetch the real power in democratiic system. how power or misuse of power transact the idea of decison making. In what way power impact responsibilityand accountability. Nexus of Power influence media to false narrative. Book illustrate thought on necessity of self actualisation for world leaders build the society together. It depicts power comes from wisdom, foundation of self actualisation learning from life failure and gather collective conscious from it to fight back; reflect the improve & better self to society. Additionally utlization of administrative thinkers theories that provide credibility of political representative.

Acknowledgements

I want to thank my mother, professors, lirary staff and others in this journey. I feel highly grateful for their motovation, constant encouragement and affirmatory helpful attitude. Yett must acknowledge the effort of Notion Press assistance team to make the whole publishing process simple and smooth.

CHAPTER ONE

RATIONALITY AND POWER

Power is nothing but it understands of self and environment. It's a feeling of self worth and personal security within, which helps taking criticism wisely and articulates into life experience. That indicates one is not giving up so easily since they want to learn how to get better. According to kautilya, "Power is strength the kind of strength which changes the mind". It identify kautilya sought the power to control inward behaviour also the thoughts of one's subjects and enemies. He explained "An arrow , discharged by an archer , may kill one person or many not kill but intellect operated by wise man possibility would kill even children in the womb." He further says, probably his science could not promise all of that but the power offered by this science was extensive.

Rationality and power are two central concepts in social, political, and psychological studies that influence human behaviour and interactions. Rationality refers to the ability to think logically, make reasoned decisions, and pursue goals based on consistent, objective, and evidence-based reasoning. It involves evaluating information, considering alternatives, and choosing actions that maximize benefits or minimize risks. Rationality is often associated with sound judgment, problem-solving, and strategic thinking.

Power, on the other hand, is the capacity to influence or control the behaviour of others, control resources, or shape outcomes in a given situation. It can be formal or informal, depending on the context, and is often derived from various sources, such as authority, wealth, knowledge, or social position. Power is a critical component of leadership, governance, and organizational dynamics, as it shapes decision-making, hierarchies, and relationships.

The relationship between rationality and power is multifaceted. Rationality can be a key driver in the acquisition and exercise of power, as individuals or groups with rational thinking tend to make more informed and effective decisions, build trust, and garner support. In turn, power can shape rationality by influencing the cognitive and emotional states of those who hold it, often leading to changes in their perceptions, biases, and decision-making processes.

Understanding the dynamic interplay between rationality and power is essential in various domains, including politics, business, and interpersonal relationships. The effective use of power often requires rationality to make decisions that balance competing interests, weigh risks, and consider long-term consequences. Conversely, rational individuals can enhance their influence and authority by leveraging their logical thinking, strategic planning, and persuasive capabilities.

However, the impact of rationality on power and vice versa can also be complex and sometimes contradictory. Power can distort rational decision-making, leading to biased, unethical, or self-serving actions, while rationality can either reinforce or challenge power structures. Therefore, exploring the role of rationality in the acquisition, use, and maintenance of power, as well as the reciprocal effects of power on rationality, is crucial for understanding human behaviour in social and organizational contexts.

As per to the Lao Tzu's simplicity, patience and compassion are greatest and brightest elements of power. Power is not always conquering or attacking instead it is a power of reflection of one kindness with patience which explored through simplicity. Our actions must express through simplicity and patience. Individual should be motivated to embrace and practise the three treats as treasure of life. Simplicity means without ego; simplicity defined as freedom from complexity intricacy or division into parts an organism of great simplicity. When there is no ego one simply gets things done. There is no ego one simply gets things done. There is no attachment, one serves and remains detached.

Patience is all about loss of temper, irritation, the quality of being patient as the bearing of provocation, annoyance misfortune or pain without complaint and suffering. Patience is the state of endurance under difficult circumstances which can means preserving in face of delay or provocation. Without holding on anger or annoyance. Especially when faced long term difficulties. When one wants quick results which gives stress to others. One probably become ignorant of others feeling & might end up hurting them. When one is impatient, one even gets angry easily.

Compassion and love is a powerful influencing tool and helps win many a heart, compassion alleviate others feelings. Motivation is the act or state of being something that motivates, inducement and incentives. Leadership can be defined as process encouraging others rather showing totaliatatism and allow to attain organizational relevant goals. Leadership is most significant force in public or private organisation, society and nation. Leaders must be aware of the power and integral use in every field of work. As a leadership is regarded as an essential element or a core value in organizational culture.

Follett identify power as leaders should value group power over individual power. Her theory suggests real power passes through the entire rather keeping to themselves After all, organisations do not exist for one person's benefit but rather for the entire company. Fayol power is more centralised neglecting manpower. According to follett, Power can never be delegated, authority can be delegated. Power exists when orders are obeyed irrespective of resistance, authority exists when orders obeyed voluntarily.

Mary also focused on the dynamics of power: power could be created and kindled or smothered and killed through the acts of authority. Real power create great leaders who take wise decision and good at setting organisational goals; as efficient leaders must be able to think strategically make informed decisions, communicate effectively, continuously learning and improving. Leaders are not just individuals who gets and give advice to others, power they are also navigators at the crossroads of choices, responsible for steering their organisation towards success.

Leadership power is not just ability to use resources and achieve organisational goals also encourage and motivate entire team to achieve organisational target together, leading entire group to achieve one ultimate goal. Power produce rationally as francis Bacon's famous tenet express as "Knowledge is power" one of the most fundamental ideas of modernity and of the enlightenment tradition the more rational Knowledge the better. Studies show that relationship between Knowledge and power is commutative, not only knowledge is power but more important power is knowledge. Power determines what gets to count as knowledge and what kind of interpretation attain authority as the dominant interpretation.

According to Herbert Simon, human beings are bounded by their cognitive limits. Human beings seek information which they don't have rather focus on their cognitive. He is widely associated with the theory of bounded rationality which states that individuals do not make perfectly rational decision because of both cognitive limits (difficulty in obtaining and processing all the information needed) and social limit (personal and social ties among individuals)

Bounded rationality basically an idea that limit the rational when individual make their own decisions, under these limitations, rational than optimal. Limitations refers to the difficulty of problem which require decision to make, cognitive availability of the mind, and the time available to make the decision. In this situation, Decision makers viewed as satisficers who seeks satisfactory decision with everything that have at the moment rather than an optimal solution. Therefore, humans do not undertake a full cost benefit analysis to determine the optimal decision, rather choose an option that satisfy their adequacy criteria.

Rationality and power" is a broad topic that can be examined in various fields such as political science, sociology, philosophy, and economics. Here's a breakdown of some key perspectives on the relationship between rationality and power:

Political Science:

Max Weber's Perspective: Weber, a German sociologist, distinguished between traditional, charismatic, and legal-rational forms of authority. He argued that modern societies tend to rely on legal-rational authority, where power is exercised through impersonal rules and procedures. Rationality, in this sense, refers to the ability to make decisions based on logical reasoning, efficiency, and systematic knowledge. However, Weber also recognized that power is not purely rational; it is often influenced by social structures and historical contingencies.

Foucault's View: Michel Foucault introduced a more dynamic understanding of power, which is not only top-down (from authority to the people) but also pervasive, operating through norms, knowledge, and social practices. Foucault viewed rationality as closely tied to power structures, as what is considered "rational" is often shaped by dominant groups or institutions. Power shapes what is considered reasonable, just, or normal in society.

Economics:

Rational Choice Theory: In economics, rationality often refers to the idea that individuals make decisions by maximizing utility based on available information. This concept assumes that individuals are logical and self-interested in their choices. Power dynamics in economics can arise when one group (e.g., corporations or governments) has more resources or information, enabling them to shape or constrain the decisions of others.

Power and Inequality: Economic power can distort rationality. For example, powerful elites may manipulate markets, economies, or political systems to benefit themselves, often masking their power with the justification of "rational" economic decisions or policies that favor the status quo.

Sociology:

Power often manifests through the control of resources, institutions, or knowledge. Rationality, in sociological terms, may be viewed as the capacity to navigate and manipulate these structures to one's advantage. Social norms and rules, often enforced by institutions (like the legal system or the media), dictate what is seen as "rational" behavior, and those in power may influence or define these norms to maintain control.

Philosophy:

Critical Theory: Philosophers like Theodor Adorno and Max Horkheimer, associated with the Frankfurt School, argue that rationality can be co-opted by systems of power. In their view, the Enlightenment's emphasis on reason and science has been appropriated by capitalist and bureaucratic institutions to dominate individuals, making rationality a tool of oppression rather than liberation.

Instrumental Rationality: Some philosophers argue that instrumental rationality (using reason to achieve specific goals) can be problematic when divorced from ethical considerations. In this view, power structures often exploit rationality for instrumental ends, leading to decisions that benefit the powerful but harm others.

Psychology:

Cognitive Biases and Power: In psychology, it is recognized that human decision-making is often influenced by biases rather than pure rationality. Power dynamics can exacerbate these biases, as those in power may shape or exploit cognitive biases to maintain control. For example, individuals in power may encourage conformity or suppress dissent by framing issues in a particular way, exploiting the cognitive biases of the masses.

Interaction Between Rationality and Power:

Legitimization of Power: Power structures often use rational arguments to justify their dominance. For example, leaders might use economic or scientific rationality to legitimize their authority, creating a narrative that their decisions are based on logical, objective reasoning, even if they serve particular interests.

Crisis of Rationality: When rationality itself is called into question, as in periods of social upheaval or intellectual critique, it may challenge the legitimacy of existing power structures. Movements that criticize dominant rationalities (such as feminism, postcolonialism, or critical theory) often aim to disrupt the ways in which power has shaped what is considered rational or normal.

In sum, rationality and power are deeply interconnected. Power influences what is considered rational, and rationality can be used as a tool to exercise or challenge power. The relationship between the two is often complex and context-dependent, with power shaping rationality and vice versa.

Political Power

Political and social power are closely related but distinct concepts that refer to the ability to influence, control, or shape the actions, behaviours, and decisions of individuals or groups. Here's a breakdown of each:

Political Power:

Political power refers to the ability to influence or control the governance of a state or political entity. It is the capacity to make and enforce laws, direct public policy, and manage public resources. Political power typically comes from holding official positions of authority or through influence over those in power.

Sources of Political Power:

Authority: Formal, legitimate power that comes from holding a political office (e.g., president, parliamentarian, mayor).

Coercion: The use of force or threats to compel others to act in a desired way (e.g., police, military).

Persuasion: The ability to shape opinions, ideas, or beliefs through rhetoric or diplomacy (e.g., politicians, activists).

Economic Power: Control over resources that can influence political decisions, such as funding for campaigns or lobbying efforts.

Cultural Influence: The role of media, education, and institutions in shaping political views.

Uses of Political Power:

Governance: Establishing laws, policies, and regulations to guide society.

Public Security: Ensuring safety and enforcing law and order.

International Relations: Engaging in diplomacy, negotiations, and defense policies.

Economic Management: Overseeing national budgets, taxation, and economic development.

Social Power:

Social power refers to the ability to influence individuals or groups in society based on relationships, social status, or cultural authority. It is not limited to formal or institutional authority but extends to various forms of influence that shape social behavior, norms, and values.

Sources of Social Power:

Social Status: Influence that comes from one's position in society (e.g., celebrities, thought leaders, high-ranking individuals).

Cultural Influence: Power derived from shaping cultural norms, values, or trends (e.g., media, arts, influencers).

Economic Power: Wealth and access to resources can elevate one's ability to influence social behaviour (e.g., business leaders, philanthropists).

Networks and Connections: Social power can come from being part of influential social groups or networks (e.g., family, professional networks, social circles).

Expertise or Knowledge: Power that stems from specialized knowledge or skills (e.g., scholars, professionals, advisors).

Uses of Social Power:

Social Movements: Influencing public opinion and behaviour toward social change (e.g., civil rights movements, environmental activism).

Cultural Change: Shaping cultural norms, values, and practices, which can redefine what's considered acceptable or desirable in society (e.g., social media trends, popular culture).

Influence over Institutions: Impacting social institutions like education, religion, and family structures.

Interconnection Between Political and Social Power:

While political power is often tied to formal positions of authority, social power operates on a more informal level, shaping the norms and behaviours of society. The two types of power frequently overlap. For example:

Political leaders often rely on social power (through public opinion or cultural influence) to gain or maintain their positions.

Social movements can transform political landscapes by using social power to create widespread demand for political change.

Overall, political power governs the structure and functioning of states, while social power shapes societal norms, behaviours, and values. Together, they can drive change, maintain order, and shape the direction of societies.

The purpose of imposing power can vary depending on the context, but generally, it involves the use of authority, influence, or control to achieve specific goals or maintain control over a situation, group, or resource. Some common reasons for imposing power include:

Maintaining Order and Stability: Governments, institutions, or organizations may impose power to enforce laws, regulations, or rules that keep order and ensure the stability of society or the organization.

Achieving Goals: Power can be used to implement policies, plans, or strategies to achieve certain objectives, whether in business, politics, or social change.

Resource Control: Power can be used to control or allocate resources (e.g., wealth, land, manpower), often to secure economic or strategic advantages.

Enforcing Ideologies: Political, religious, or social leaders might impose power to spread or maintain a particular ideology or belief system.

Defending Against Threats: Imposing power may be necessary for defense, whether in response to external aggression, internal disorder, or competition.

Influence and Manipulation: Sometimes power is used for manipulation, where individuals or groups use authority or control to influence the behavior or decisions of others for personal gain.

In each case, the ethical implications of imposing power depend on how it is done, its fairness, and the consequences for those who are affected by it.

Power can have a significant influence on rationality, shaping decision-making and cognitive processes in both positive and negative ways. Here are some key ways power influences rationality:

Overconfidence and Bias: Individuals in positions of power often develop overconfidence in their abilities and decisions. This overconfidence can impair rationality by leading to riskier decisions and ignoring contrary evidence. Power can create a sense of invulnerability, resulting in biased thinking where a person may discount the perspectives of others, especially those who are less powerful.

Social Distance: Power can create psychological distance between those in authority and those under their influence. This social distance might reduce empathy and hinder the ability to understand others' perspectives, leading to decisions that may not be fully rational or considerate of all relevant information.

Reduced Cognitive Load: Research suggests that people in positions of power often have greater cognitive resources available. Power can decrease the stress and cognitive load that typically accompanies decision-making in lower positions, leading to more streamlined and efficient processing of information. However, this can also lead to over-simplification, causing them to overlook complexities.

Moral Licensing: Power can lead to a phenomenon called moral licensing, where individuals in power may feel justified in making decisions that serve their own interests at the expense of others. The sense of entitlement that power can bring might weaken moral reasoning, potentially leading to less rational or ethical decisions.

In-group Bias: Those in power may be more prone to favoring those within their own group or circle, leading to a bias in decision-making. This in-group favoritism can distort rational decision-making by prioritizing loyalty or personal interests over objective considerations.

Risk Tolerance: Power can influence risk tolerance, often leading those in power to take more significant risks. Their rationality might be compromised as they are more willing to accept uncertainty or make bold, high-stakes decisions without adequately weighing the potential consequences.

In sum, while power can enable more efficient decision-making in some cases, it can also skew rationality in ways that are self-serving, biased, and less considerate of broader perspectives or ethical concerns.

Rationality can also significantly influence the acquisition and exercise of power. Here are some ways in which rationality impacts power:

Strategic Decision-Making: Rationality enables individuals or groups to make more calculated, thoughtful decisions. When making strategic decisions, those who are rational are better able to evaluate situations, consider long-term consequences, and weigh risks and benefits, which can improve their ability to acquire and maintain power. In competitive environments, rational decision-making allows for better positioning and resource allocation, increasing the likelihood of success.

Effective Problem Solving: Rational individuals are often skilled at identifying and solving problems, which is crucial for those in leadership or powerful positions. Problem-solving abilities enhance one's reputation and competence, fostering trust and confidence from others. This can increase one's influence and power, as people are more likely to follow those they perceive as competent and capable.

Persuasion and Influence: Rationality often plays a key role in persuasion. A rational argument, supported by logic and evidence, is more likely to convince others and gain support. Power is frequently derived from the ability to persuade others, whether it's convincing a group to support a particular cause, leading negotiations, or influencing public opinion. Rationality helps in presenting clear and compelling arguments that enhance one's influence.

Ethical Leadership: Rational decision-making allows leaders to consider the ethical implications of their actions and balance competing interests. Ethical leadership can be a source of legitimate power, as individuals or groups are more likely to support those who make decisions that are fair, just, and aligned with moral principles. Rationality helps in navigating complex ethical dilemmas and ensuring that power is exercised responsibly.

Emotional Regulation and Impulse Control: Rational individuals often have greater control over their emotions and impulses. This emotional regulation helps them make more objective, less reactive decisions, especially in high-pressure situations. Leaders with better impulse control can maintain authority, avoid rash decisions, and manage crises effectively, all of which contribute to sustaining and increasing their power.

Adaptability and Learning: Rationality involves the capacity for learning and adapting based on new information. Individuals who approach situations with a rational mindset are more likely to adjust their strategies and behaviors when necessary, which helps them navigate changing circumstances. This adaptability can enhance power, as it allows individuals to maintain or increase their influence in dynamic environments.

Long-Term Planning: Rationality often involves the ability to think long-term and consider future consequences. Leaders or individuals in power who adopt a long-term perspective are better positioned to build lasting influence, plan for future success, and prevent short-term decisions that might undermine their power later on.

However, it's important to note that while rationality can significantly bolster power, it can also be a double-edged sword. Overly rational decision-makers might become detached from emotional or human factors that influence power dynamics, or they might use their rationality to manipulate situations for self-serving purposes. Therefore, the relationship between rationality and power can be complex and context-dependent.

The Relationship Between Rationality and Power:

Rationality as a Tool for Power: Those who possess power often use rationality as a tool to achieve and maintain their position. Political leaders, organizations, and social groups may use logical strategies and data to consolidate their influence, make decisions, and craft policies that align with their interests. Rational decision-making can enhance the effectiveness of power by making it more predictable and sustainable.

Power's Influence on Rationality: Conversely, power dynamics can shape and sometimes limit rationality. Individuals or groups with power may impose their interpretations of what is "rational," which may not always align with objective logic or collective well-being. In situations of power imbalance, those in power may use it to dictate what is considered rational or logical, influencing the decision-making processes of others. This can lead to the suppression of dissenting opinions, the manipulation of information, or the distortion of rational analysis.

Limits of Rationality in Power: While rationality can lead to efficient and effective use of power, it is not always the determining factor. Power often involves emotional, cultural, or ethical dimensions that go beyond purely rational calculations. For example, populist leaders may appeal to emotions and beliefs rather than rational arguments to maintain or expand their power.

Conclusion:

Rationality and power are deeply intertwined, with rational thinking often facilitating the strategic exercise of power, while power can also shape and limit rationality. While rationality can help optimize the use of power, the exercise of power often transcends mere logic, encompassing human emotions, social dynamics, and ethical considerations. The relationship between the two shapes the decisions, actions, and outcomes that define both individual lives and the functioning of societies. Rationality and power are deeply interconnected concepts that influence both individual and collective behaviour, as well as the structure and functioning of societies. Rationality involves the use of reason, logic, and strategic thinking to make decisions, often with the aim of achieving specific goals or optimizing outcomes. It is typically associated with the pursuit of efficiency and the application of knowledge to navigate complex situations.

CHAPTER TWO

Decision making and Power

The concept of bounded rationality complements the idea of rationality as optimization which views decision making as a fully rational process of finding an optimal choice given the information available. Therefore, bounded rationality can be said to address the discrepancy between the assumed perfect rationality of human behaviour and reality of human cognition. Bounded rationality emphasizes on perfectly rational decisions are often not feasible in practice because of the intractability of natural decisions problems.

When we think with our cognitive rational then it's automatically created power ; power is not about imposing own point of views on others infact it is about keeping everyone together with exercise of power. Individuals and groups with the capacity to define rationality have the power to influence the actions of large groups of people. Real rationality is the freedom to interpret and use, "rationality " and "rationalization" for the purpose of power. This is a crucial element in enabling power to define reality and hence, an essential feature of the rationality of power. One of the privileges of power and an integral part of its rationality is the freedom to define reality. The greater the power the greater the freedom in their respect and less need for power to understand, how reality is really constructed. Foucault says rationality as rationalization resulted in the fragmentation of the project.

Often politicians abuse the power in the form of malfeasance in office is the commission of a lawful act, done in an official capacity. Power does not exclusively refer to the threat or use of force by one actor against another but may also be exerted through. Ability of understanding other must be consider as real power. Influencing others in a way that change their perspective to think concluded as real power. Referent power is the power or ability of individual to attract others and build loyalty. It is based on charisma and interpersonal skills of the power holder. A person may be admired because of specific personal trait, expert power is an individual' power serving from the skills or expertise of the person and the organisation's needs for those skills and expertise. Unlike the others, this type of power is usually highly specific and limited to the particular area in which expert is trained And qualified. Power is one of the most contested concepts in social and political theory.

Rationalize decision build power which benefit others rather exploiting others, high power people have more self confidence than low power people and over confidence will make them biased decisions. Strategic decision making should be rationally bounded; power win battle of choice. The strategic decision making process involves every nation or company in the world exists along with other nations or companies none can exist in isolation. Different nations and companies have different national or market interest that probably clash. This leads each nation or company to feel threatened by other nations or companies. Decision makers need to find out the extent of the threat or competition which their nation or companies faces from the others.

Once the threat is asserted, strategies or course of action (COA) are generated to meet it and to achieve strategic objective within the framework of execution of doctrine. Large number of strategies have evolved these have to be evaluated in terms of the future scenario and best is chosen and executed. To choose those strategies which can cater for future crisis and contingency situations. Decision making needs guidance or at least some form of mechanism.

Strategic decision making brings the important information about evaluation and development of environment inside and outside the company and reveals possible opportunities and threat that need to be consider in strategic decision making. There is always an interest to improve strategic decision making among both managers and researchers. Interest in improving and strategic decision making is related to change in current environment and to the difficulty that managers have to face in decision making nowadays. As we aware, environment is constantly change which directly or indirectly impact the decision making. Changes are much frequent which previous generations of entrepreneurs' and managers did align with. Changes can bring new opportunities for companies development.

Decision making influenced by many factors and require theories and practice to develop the wise decisions. Rational decision create power to improve the life of others this kind of power mostly found in political arena when political leaders either use their power or misuse their power. For many managers the most difficult part is forecasting and assessing of the implemented strategic variants because of different dynamic exists in environment.

For many managers, the most difficult part is forecasting and assessing consequences of the implemented strategic variants because dynamicity of environment. Decision making and power refers to the direct relationship between the ability to make choices and the influence or control one holds over a situation or group of people. Individuals with ultimate power may directly impose their choices on others with the consideration of others and opinions. People with power take risks due to a perception of greater control and less accountability, powerful individuals access more information or be able to selectively share information to influence decisions in their favour. Large engagement in decision making processes.

It can increase their sense of agency and power within a group. Participatory decision making can distribute power more evenly and lead to more inclusive outcome. By making informed and well reasoned decisions, individuals can challenge the power dynamic within a system. One of the most important aspects of decision making is the ability to assess risks and rewards. Every decision we make involves some level of risk and the best decision makers are those who can accurately evaluate the potential risks and rewards of each option. The ability to make sound decisions is a critical skills that can determine the success and failure of an individual or organization. Another important aspect of decision making is the ability to think critically and logically.

The best decisions are made by individuals who can approach a problem with an open mind and carefully evaluate all the available information. The power of decision making extends beyond the individual level and can have a significant impact on organisation and society as a whole. The same applies to the decisions made by corporate leaders which can impact the success or failure of entire companies. Therefore, the ability to make sound decisions is an essential skills for leaders at all levels. Strategic decision makers are boundedly rational that power wins battles of choice and that chance matters. People who holds high power make more conservative decisions however, circumstances changes in which the dominance of hierarchy was unstable and more likely to lose their powers. When power was irrevocable and participants choices had no bearing on their ability to retain power both high and low power motivated participants responded by making riskier decisions.

Some scholars focuses on cognitive aspect of decision making and discussed nine indicators of competence, choice, comprehension, creativity, compromise, consequentiality, correctness, credibility consistency and commitment. Power should be exercised in decentralised way. Decision making needs to be considerate in decentralised manner to achieve the goal of organisation. Decision making must not passes through in hierarchical manner, it should be more flexible than presence as rigid. Right decision making not let to misuse of power infact it dictate more open way working in the organisation.

Decision making, rationality, leadership are few elements that determine capacity of power. Decision making is most important trait if individual personality and exercising the different level of power. Power cannot ensure in centralised, it is like more learning from the environment and take decision accordingly. Decision making is the same to conclude the power. Individual can enjoy power only when it's not absolute to one rather it flows within the organisation for all people.

Power is output of perfect decision making, Decision makers possibly establish their cognitive Intellect to solve the problem, power can only attain by engagement and involvement of people. Power is a source of wise decision making; Decision making and leadership go hand and hand to get the power to fulfill the goal of the organisations. Decision making processes aim to gain the confidence of the people in the organisation to get the full control on the resources. Once we have control on the resources, it will be easier to attain the power. Rationality is a another key source of power which helps to improve the overall performance of the organisation. According to M P Follett, there should be engagement of management with subordinate where there is no disparity on the hierarchical level. Negligence of hierarchy structure is essential to navigate the organisational goals. Leadership emergency power hence, leadership plays vital role in attain power which can be useful for organization.

Leaders must embrace the concept of "engagement leadership" which involves all aspects of the organisation and maintain harmony with the environment through leadership. Follett, emphasizes on the role of the leaders with their subordinates which follows bottom to up of the hierarchical structure. Follett explained power as distinct feature of the power over and power with. "Power might be defined as simple ability to make things happen, to be casual agent to initiate change". Power over is coercive power while other define as coactive power. Power with is a self developing entity which promotes better understanding, reduces friction and conflict and encourage cooperative action and promote participative decision making. (Metcalf and Urwick, 1940)

Absolute power make individual dictator rather emergency as leader , keeping and taking all individual of the organisation in one pack consider as significant step towards building a true leader. True leader identify as when decision making is dealing with all together. Political factors heavily shape decision making within world organisation as diverse national interests, power dynamics and leadership style came into play. These factors influence the agenda, policies and effectiveness of international organisations.

Both decision making and leadership are vital trait to claim the power, decision making influence the policy formulation and any organisation. Political factors are cautionly effect the misuse of power. Decision making allow to work cohesively and achieving organisation goal. Decision making and power are two face of one coin, one cannot complete without other. Decision making efficiency determine by power being utilised in the process. Policy making and implementation ensure or guarantee through decision making. Decision making effectively determine degree of power; if decision making goes wrong then one can say power was not utilized consciously.

Decision making has huge impact on individual as well as on the goal of the organisation. Abuse of power is easy on hierarchical level. Hierarchy often use power in excessive manner which can lead to misuse of the power. Effectiveness of the organisation and it's goal significantly depend on the power of decision making. Power can be misuse if decision making is not efficiently used. True leaders' qualities are decision making, rationality which can helpful to determine power and leadership. In this context, power cannot be used vaguely.

Power and decision-making are closely interconnected concepts in both organizational and personal contexts. Power refers to the ability or capacity to influence others, control resources, or enforce decisions. It shapes the way decisions are made and can determine whose interests are considered in the process. Decision-making is the process of selecting a course of action from a set of alternatives. Here's how power and decision-making interact:

1. Types of Power in Decision-Making:

Legitimate Power: Power derived from a formal position or role within an organization. Those with legitimate power often make important decisions and influence others' actions.

Expert Power: Power based on knowledge or expertise. Decision-makers with specialized knowledge are often consulted or relied upon for their input in decision-making processes.

Referent Power: Power that comes from the ability to attract others due to qualities such as charisma, trust, or respect. This can influence group decision-making.

Coercive Power: Power based on the ability to punish or control through negative consequences. It can shape decision outcomes by threatening undesirable actions.

Reward Power: The ability to grant rewards or benefits, which can be used to influence the decision-making process of others.

2. Influence on Decision-Making:

Top-Down Decision Making: In hierarchical organizations, leaders with significant power typically make critical decisions, directing others to follow.

Collaborative Decision Making: Power can be distributed among groups, allowing for shared input and consensus-building, which can lead to more inclusive decisions.

Centralized vs. Decentralized Decision-Making: In centralized systems, power is concentrated at the top, where decisions are made by a few individuals. In decentralized systems, decision-making power is spread across various levels, leading to more autonomy at lower levels of the organization.

3. Power Imbalances in Decision-Making:

Concentration of Power: When too much power is held by one individual or group, it can lead to biased or unfair decision-making, as their interests might dominate the process.

Resistance and Conflict: In cases of power disparity, those with less power may resist decisions or take actions to challenge authority, potentially leading to conflict and a breakdown in decision-making.

Ethical Considerations: Power dynamics can affect fairness and equity in decision-making. Those in power may prioritize their own interests over the common good, leading to ethical dilemmas.

4. The Role of Power in Organizational Decision-Making:

Strategic Decisions: Leaders use their power to make high-level, strategic decisions that guide the direction of the organization.

Operational Decisions: Lower-level managers or teams may have the power to make day-to-day decisions, although these are still influenced by the broader strategic choices made by higher-level executives.

Political Dynamics: Power struggles and political tactics often influence decision-making, as various factions within an organization seek to protect their interests or gain advantages.

5. Improving Decision-Making in Power Structures:

Transparency: Decision-making processes should be clear and open to ensure that power is exercised fairly and responsibly.

Empowerment: Encouraging distributed power, where individuals or groups at all levels have a say in decisions, can lead to more democratic and effective decision-making.

Conflict Resolution: Addressing power imbalances and promoting healthy debate can prevent poor decisions and foster a more inclusive decision-making environment.

Power significantly impacts decision-making by shaping who gets to participate, whose voices are heard, and the outcomes of the decisions. Decision-making is a crucial process in both personal and professional contexts. Its importance lies in the following areas:

Achieving Goals: Effective decision-making enables individuals and organizations to make choices that align with their long-term objectives and desired outcomes, increasing the likelihood of success.

Problem Solving: Making decisions is key to solving problems, whether they are immediate challenges or complex, long-term issues. It helps in analyzing options and choosing the most appropriate course of action.

Resource Allocation: Good decisions lead to better utilization of resources—time, money, and human capital—ensuring that efforts are directed toward productive and efficient outcomes.

Risk Management: Effective decision-making involves assessing potential risks and benefits, which helps in minimizing negative consequences while maximizing opportunities.

Building Confidence: When decisions lead to positive outcomes, they build confidence in leaders and individuals, helping them take further calculated actions in future situations.

Improving Adaptability: With the fast-changing nature of the world, being able to make timely and informed decisions allows individuals and organizations to adapt quickly to new circumstances.

In essence, decision-making influences success, growth, and the ability to navigate through complex environments.

Leadership plays a crucial role in decision-making for several reasons:

Vision and Direction: Effective leaders provide a clear vision and direction, helping guide the decision-making process. Their ability to align decisions with long-term goals ensures that choices are made with the bigger picture in mind.

Influence and Motivation: Leaders inspire and motivate their teams, encouraging collaboration and buy-in for decisions. When leaders demonstrate confidence in their choices, it often strengthens team commitment to those decisions.

Problem-Solving: Leaders are often required to navigate complex situations. Their experience, wisdom, and ability to analyze various factors allow them to make well-informed decisions, often under pressure.

Risk Management: A strong leader can assess potential risks and rewards, balancing caution with boldness. They can steer the team through uncertainty and mitigate negative impacts.

Accountability: Effective leaders take responsibility for their decisions, ensuring accountability. This builds trust within the organization and motivates others to take ownership of their actions.

Ethical Decision-Making: Leadership sets the tone for ethical behavior. A leader's decisions often serve as a model for the rest of the organization, influencing how others approach decision-making, especially in challenging situations.

leadership is vital in decision-making as it provides clarity, accountability, and direction, ensuring that decisions support the broader goals of the organization while maintaining motivation and ethical integrity.

CHAPTER THREE

PUBLIC POLICY AND POWER

Public policy refers to the actions and decisions made by government authorities to address societal issues or problems. It encompasses laws, regulations, programs, and actions that aim to improve public welfare, manage resources, and address challenges such as education, healthcare, the environment, and economic stability. Public policies are often shaped by political, social, economic, and cultural factors and are designed to respond to the needs of the population.

In the policymaking process, governments typically identify problems, set goals, develop strategies, implement policies, and evaluate outcomes. Public policies are influenced by a variety of stakeholders, including elected officials, political parties, interest groups, and citizens, and can be dynamic, evolving over time to reflect changes in society, technology, or public opinion.

Public policy can be classified into different categories such as social policy (focused on health, welfare, education), economic policy (concerning fiscal and monetary issues), environmental policy (dealing with sustainability and climate change), and foreign policy (governing relations with other nations). Effective public policy requires balancing competing interests and ensuring that solutions are both fair and sustainable for the long term:

Power in politics refers to the ability of individuals, groups, or institutions to influence or control the behavior, actions, and decisions of others within a political system. It is a fundamental concept in political science, as it shapes the dynamics between governments, citizens, and various political actors. Political power can manifest in different forms, such as:

Coercive Power: The use of force or the threat of force, often seen in authoritarian regimes or during times of conflict.

Legitimate Power: Authority granted through formal institutions like laws, constitutions, and democratic elections, where power is perceived as right or justified.

Economic Power: Control over resources, wealth, and economic systems that can influence political decisions, often wielded by corporations, elites, or financial institutions.

Ideological Power: The ability to shape beliefs, values, and ideologies, often through media, education, and political discourse.

Power is central to politics because it dictates who makes decisions, how resources are allocated, and how policies affect societies. It can be exercised at various levels: local, national, or international, and it plays a key role in the balance between democracy and autocracy, equality and inequality. Understanding power dynamics is crucial for analyzing political behavior, institutions, and the outcomes of political processes.

Politicians influence public policy in several ways:

Legislation: Elected officials, especially lawmakers, draft, propose, and pass laws that shape public policy. This includes creating new laws, amending existing ones, and responding to societal issues. For example, politicians in the U.S. Congress can introduce bills that directly affect areas like healthcare, education, and environmental regulations.

Advocacy and Campaigning: Politicians often use their platform to advocate for specific policies. They campaign for issues they believe in, which may include reforms, government spending priorities, or social changes. By influencing public opinion, they can push for the adoption of certain policies.

Executive Orders and Actions: Presidents, governors, and other executives can issue executive orders or take administrative actions to implement certain policies. For example, a president may use an executive order to address immigration policy or environmental regulations without needing legislative approval.

Public Influence and Opinion: Politicians leverage their status to shape public opinion, often through speeches, media appearances, or social media. Public support or opposition can lead to changes in policy, as elected officials respond to the desires and concerns of their constituents.

Lobbying and Relationships with Interest Groups: Politicians may work with interest groups, think tanks, or political action committees (PACs) that lobby for specific policy changes. They may receive campaign donations or support in exchange for advocating for policies that benefit these groups.

International Diplomacy: Politicians at the national level, particularly heads of state, influence international public policy through treaties, negotiations, and foreign relations. These policies can affect trade, security, and environmental standards globally.

Votebank politics refers to a political strategy where political parties or leaders focus on securing the votes of specific demographic, social, or religious groups to win elections. This strategy often involves catering to the interests, needs, and concerns of these groups, sometimes by offering targeted policies, welfare schemes, or promises that align with their preferences. The goal is to consolidate a large, reliable group of voters who will consistently support a particular party or candidate.

In countries like India, votebank politics can involve appealing to caste, religion, region, or community-based groups. Political parties may seek to create alliances or adopt rhetoric that resonates with these groups to maintain or enhance their electoral support. However, this can sometimes lead to divisiveness, as it may foster a sense of competition or even animosity between different groups, emphasizing identity over broader national or policy-based considerations.

The key elements of votebank politics are:

Identity-based mobilization: Using social or cultural identity (such as caste, religion, or language) to gather support.

Targeted promises: Making policy promises or decisions that directly benefit a particular group.

Polarization: Often, this strategy can deepen social divisions, as parties may focus more on appealing to their base rather than promoting inclusive development.

While votebank politics may be effective in gaining votes in the short term, it can also undermine social harmony and promote division in society.

Through these methods, politicians can directly or indirectly shape how society is governed and which issues get prioritized.

Politicians often focus on votebank politics as a strategy to secure electoral success. Votebank politics involves catering to specific groups of voters based on factors like religion, caste, ethnicity, or economic class, rather than promoting policies for the broader population. Here's why they may focus on it:

Targeted Appeal: By focusing on particular groups, politicians can ensure loyalty from these communities, leading to concentrated votes. If a politician or party can guarantee the support of a strong votebank, it becomes easier to win elections.

Appeasement: Politicians may offer specific benefits or promises tailored to the needs and desires of a particular group to gain their votes. This could involve welfare schemes, reservations, or other targeted policies.

Polarization: Sometimes, politicians use divisive tactics to reinforce group identities, creating "us vs. them" narratives to solidify their vote bank. This strategy can rally people based on common identity, fear, or historical grievances.

Resource Allocation: Politicians may direct resources to constituencies with strong votebanks, ensuring they fulfill the expectations of those groups. This could be in the form of government jobs, subsidies, or infrastructure development.

Emotional Appeal: By emphasizing identity politics, politicians can evoke strong emotional responses that help consolidate their support base. This makes it difficult for opposing candidates to sway those voters.

In the long run, this focus on votebank politics may deepen societal divides, prioritizing short-term electoral gains over long-term national development and unity. It often results in policies that may benefit a few groups but fail to address broader national issues.

Excessive power influencing public policy can have significant consequences, often undermining democratic principles, fairness, and public trust. When power is concentrated in the hands of a few individuals, corporations, or interest groups, they can manipulate or skew policy decisions to benefit their own agendas rather than serving the broader public interest.

Here are a few ways excessive power can affect public policy:

Policy Capture: Powerful corporations or special interest groups can exert undue influence over legislators or regulators, resulting in policies that prioritize their interests over the needs of ordinary citizens. This can lead to regulations that benefit big businesses or wealthy elites, while neglecting the welfare of the general public.

Lack of Accountability: When influential entities hold sway over policy decisions, it can reduce transparency and accountability. Decision-making becomes more opaque, and citizens may feel that their voices aren't being heard, eroding trust in government institutions.

Economic Inequality: The influence of powerful interest groups can contribute to policies that favor the rich and powerful, exacerbating economic inequality. Tax cuts for the wealthy, deregulation of industries, or corporate-friendly trade deals can further concentrate wealth and resources in the hands of a few.

Corruption: Excessive power often leads to corruption, where decision-makers may be bribed or otherwise incentivized to pass laws that benefit specific individuals or companies. This can result in skewed policies that harm public welfare.

Undermining Democracy: When powerful entities have too much influence over policy, the voice of the people can be drowned out. This undermines democratic processes, where ideally, policy decisions should reflect the will of the majority rather than the interests of a select few.

To address excessive power's influence on public policy, it's important to promote transparency, campaign finance reforms, lobbying regulations, and encourage civic engagement to ensure that policies serve the common good.

Public policy typically consists of several key components that work together to address societal issues or achieve specific goals. These components include:

Policy Agenda: This refers to the issues or topics that are prioritized by decision-makers, reflecting the public's concerns, political realities, and institutional agendas.

Policy Formulation: This is the stage where potential solutions or courses of action are developed. Experts, lawmakers, and stakeholders work together to design the policies that could address the identified issues.

Policy Adoption: In this phase, policymakers, such as legislators or government officials, make decisions on which policy to implement. This often involves debates, voting, and negotiations.

Policy Implementation: After a policy is adopted, this step involves putting the policy into action. It typically involves government agencies, organizations, and other stakeholders carrying out the plans and programs established.

Policy Evaluation: This component involves assessing the effectiveness of the policy. Policymakers review the outcomes, analyze data, and determine whether the policy achieved its intended goals or needs adjustment.

Policy Modification or Termination: Based on evaluation, a policy may be adjusted or reformed. If it is not effective or if new issues arise, a policy can be reformed, modified, or even repealed.

These components interact in a cyclical process, and the success of public policy depends on how effectively each part is executed.

Politics plays a crucial role in shaping public policy because political leaders and parties make decisions that directly affect how policies are created, implemented, and evaluated. The impact of politics on public policy can be seen in several ways:

Policy Formulation: Political ideologies, party platforms, and the priorities of elected officials often dictate the types of policies that are proposed. For example, a liberal or progressive government may prioritize social welfare programs, while a conservative government may focus on reducing taxes and limiting government intervention.

Political Influence and Lobbying: Interest groups, corporations, and other stakeholders often lobby politicians to influence public policy in their favor. This can lead to the creation of policies that serve the interests of certain groups rather than the broader public.

Political Gridlock and Compromise: Political polarization and division within government can result in gridlock, where little progress is made on important policy issues. In such environments, public policy may either stagnate or become a series of compromises that may not fully address the needs of society.

Public Opinion and Voting Behavior: Political leaders often craft policies to align with the views and demands of their constituents, which can influence public policy decisions. The need to win elections and maintain power leads politicians to design policies that cater to the preferences of voters.

Economic and Social Policies: Governments' political decisions can impact a country's economic direction—taxation, spending, and trade policies—and social policies, such as education, healthcare, and welfare. Political agendas shape how these issues are approached, affecting the distribution of resources and opportunities within society.

Changes in Leadership: Shifts in political leadership, such as new presidents or prime ministers, can lead to significant changes in public policy. A change in political leadership often brings a change in focus, with new priorities and policy directions.

Overall, the political landscape heavily influences public policy, as decisions are made based on political considerations, values, and agendas. These political dynamics shape the policies that affect people's daily lives, from healthcare to education to economic opportunities.

Self-actualization and power are concepts that can be linked in a variety of ways, depending on the context in which they are discussed.

Self-actualization refers to the realization of one's full potential, which is a key concept in Maslow's hierarchy of needs. It's the process of becoming the best version of oneself, often involving personal growth, self-discovery, and the pursuit of meaning. Individuals who are self-actualized are often described as being authentic, self-aware, and driven by intrinsic goals rather than external validation.

Power, on the other hand, can refer to the ability to influence, control, or direct others and situations. It often involves authority, control, or influence in social, political, or professional contexts.

While self-actualization is more internally driven, power can be seen as something that is often exerted externally. However, these two concepts can intersect in the following ways:

Internal Power: A self-actualized person often has a strong sense of internal power. This is the confidence, self-awareness, and inner strength that allows them to live authentically, make decisions based on their values, and influence their environment in a way that aligns with their purpose.

External Power: As someone becomes more self-actualized, they may naturally acquire more external power. This could manifest in leadership roles, where they inspire others through their example, or in their ability to create meaningful change in their environment due to their clarity of vision and purpose.

Balance of Power: Self-actualization involves understanding the importance of balance—acknowledging both the power one has within themselves and the power dynamics that exist in the outside world. An individual who is self-actualized may not seek power for its own sake, but they may use the power they have in ways that are responsible and aligned with their values.

In essence, self-actualization can give someone a deeper sense of personal power, but true power in the external world often requires interpersonal skills, strategic thinking, and a level of social influence that can take time to develop. The most empowering path is usually one where power is wielded responsibly, driven by a sense of purpose, and aligned with personal values.

CHAPTER FOUR

RESPONSIBILITY AND POWER

Politicians generate power through a combination of various strategies, resources, and circumstances. Here are some of the key ways they acquire and maintain power:

Electoral Support: One of the most direct ways politicians generate power is by winning elections. They appeal to the electorate through campaigns that resonate with voters' needs, desires, and beliefs. Building a strong voter base is crucial.

Political Parties and Alliances: Politicians often align with political parties or form alliances to gain more influence. Being part of a larger political network provides access to resources, funding, and a broad base of support.

Policy and Ideology: Developing clear, appealing policies and an ideological stance helps politicians gain supporters and build loyalty. By addressing public concerns (e.g., economy, security, healthcare), they can gain the trust and support needed for power.

Charismatic Leadership: Some politicians generate power through personal charisma. They inspire and connect emotionally with the public, creating a sense of trust and loyalty. Charisma can often amplify a politician's influence beyond their immediate political party.

Control of Resources: Political power is often closely tied to access to resources—be it economic, social, or institutional. Politicians who can control or distribute resources (such as government contracts, jobs, or funding) often gain leverage over others.

Institutional Power: Once in office, politicians can generate power by occupying positions that give them significant authority, such as roles in the executive, legislature, or judiciary. They can also use their influence within bureaucratic systems to advance their goals.

Public Speaking and Media: Modern politicians use media—whether traditional, like TV and radio, or social media platforms—to communicate with the public, shape their image, and push their agendas. Strategic media appearances can amplify their influence.

Manipulation and Negotiation: Behind the scenes, politicians often gain power through negotiation, making deals, or even manipulating rivals or allies. This includes forming coalitions, making compromises, and leveraging influence in legislative or diplomatic settings.

Perception of Competence or Crisis Management: In times of crisis (economic downturns, national security threats, natural disasters), politicians who can present themselves as competent and capable leaders gain credibility and power. Public perception of effectiveness plays a significant role in securing and maintaining power.

Building a Legacy: Some politicians generate long-term power by leaving behind significant achievements or reforms that impact society positively, ensuring they are remembered and respected. This often translates into continued influence even after their term in office.

Power generation, in essence, is a combination of personal skills, strategic alliances, institutional resources, and public support, all influenced by the political and societal context in which the politician operates.

Politicians generate both power and responsibility through a balance of actions, strategies, and ethical leadership. While power gives them the ability to influence and make decisions, responsibility holds them accountable for the outcomes of those decisions. Here's how they balance these two elements:

1. Accountability to Voters

Power: Politicians gain power through electoral victories, winning the trust of the electorate, and forming political alliances.

Responsibility: With that power comes the responsibility to act in the best interest of their constituents. They must answer to the people who elected them, ensuring their policies align with the public's needs and values. This accountability ensures that the power isn't misused.

2. Ethical Decision-Making

Power: Politicians are in positions where they can make laws, allocate resources, and influence public policy.

Responsibility: They are responsible for making decisions that are ethical, transparent, and fair. This includes ensuring that their policies benefit society as a whole and don't favor special interests over the public good. Effective leaders balance the power they hold with moral and ethical considerations.

3. Building Trust and Credibility

Power: Politicians acquire power by building a credible reputation, delivering on promises, and showcasing their ability to lead effectively.

Responsibility: With trust comes responsibility. Politicians must ensure they are transparent, honest, and follow through on campaign promises. When politicians break trust, they lose their power. Maintaining credibility and fulfilling promises is key to preserving both power and responsibility.

4. Policy Implementation and Consequences

Power: With political power comes the ability to shape policy and laws that can impact many areas, from the economy to healthcare and education.

Responsibility: Politicians are responsible for the consequences of their policies. They must anticipate the effects of their decisions on various groups and communities, ensuring that the laws and policies they pass lead to positive outcomes and are adaptable to unforeseen circumstances.

5. Public Service and Advocacy

Power: Politicians wield power by representing the needs of their constituents in government, advocating for laws, budgets, and reforms.

Responsibility: They have the responsibility to advocate for and serve the people who elected them, rather than using their power for personal gain or partisan advantage. A politician's responsibility is to work for the public good and prioritize long-term benefits over short-term political gain.

6. Collaboration and Compromise

Power: A politician in power can influence legislative bodies, executive decisions, and public discourse.

Responsibility: However, they must recognize the responsibility to collaborate with others, including those with differing views. Effective leadership requires listening to different perspectives, reaching compromises, and working towards solutions that serve the greater good. Balancing power with responsibility involves avoiding authoritarianism and respecting democratic processes.

7. Institutional Checks and Balances

Power: Politicians hold power through elected office, government positions, or leadership roles within parties and institutions.

Responsibility: They must respect the checks and balances inherent in democratic systems, understanding that their power is limited and subject to oversight. Ensuring responsible use of power requires adherence to laws, regulations, and ethical standards.

8. Transparency and Communication

Power: Politicians often have access to information, decision-making processes, and public platforms, enabling them to influence public opinion and policy.

Responsibility: Politicians must be transparent about their decisions and policies, communicating openly with the public about their goals, challenges, and the reasoning behind their choices. This helps them maintain trust and align their actions with the public's expectations.

9. Leadership During Crises

Power: In times of crisis (e.g., natural disasters, economic downturns), politicians have the power to mobilize resources, lead emergency responses, and implement rapid changes.

Responsibility: With that power, they have the responsibility to lead effectively, prioritize public safety, and ensure equitable distribution of resources. Their leadership must be guided by empathy, data, and a focus on long-term recovery rather than short-term political benefits.

10. Long-Term Vision

Power: Politicians often have the power to shape the future through long-term policies related to infrastructure, education, and the economy.

Responsibility: They must balance their immediate political ambitions with long-term societal impact. Decisions made in the present must consider future generations, ensuring that the power used today does not harm future progress or create unsustainable burdens.

In summary, the balance between power and responsibility for politicians is rooted in ethical leadership, accountability, and a commitment to public service. While power allows politicians to shape policy and influence change, responsibility requires them to act with integrity, respect democratic processes, and prioritize the well-being of the public they serve. Both elements must work together for effective and just governance.

Power and responsibility are closely interconnected, often viewed as two sides of the same coin. Power refers to the ability or capacity to influence, control, or direct others or events. Responsibility, on the other hand, refers to the obligation to act ethically, be accountable for one's actions, and address the consequences of those actions.

When power is exercised without responsibility, it can lead to abuse, injustice, or harm. This is because the person or group wielding the power may act in their own interest without regard for the welfare of others or the broader impact. However, when power is coupled with responsibility, it fosters a balance where individuals or institutions use their power to make positive, ethical decisions and work toward the greater good, taking accountability for the outcomes.

A popular saying, "With great power comes great responsibility," captures the idea that those who have power—whether in leadership, influence, or resources—must recognize and manage the consequences of their actions, using their influence for positive outcomes rather than self-interest or harm. The relationship between power and responsibility is essential for maintaining trust, fairness, and justice in any society or organization.

Responsibility strengthens power by fostering trust, accountability, and respect from others. When a person takes responsibility for their actions, decisions, and outcomes, they demonstrate reliability and competence, which in turn builds credibility and authority. Here's how it works:

Trust and Respect: People are more likely to follow and support someone who takes responsibility for their actions. When leaders or individuals own up to their mistakes and successes, they earn the trust and respect of others, which is crucial for exerting influence and gaining power.

Accountability: With responsibility comes accountability. When individuals or leaders are held accountable for their actions, they are more inclined to make thoughtful, strategic decisions, which can lead to better outcomes. This consistent performance builds their influence and increases their power.

Effective Decision-Making: Responsibility requires careful consideration and thoughtfulness, especially in complex situations. Those who take responsibility are often more intentional with their decisions, strengthening their position by making wise, informed choices that lead to positive results.

Leadership Development: Taking responsibility is essential for effective leadership. A responsible leader inspires confidence in their followers, showing that they can handle challenges and navigate difficult situations, which ultimately strengthens their power and influence over time.

Self-empowerment: Responsibility also empowers the individual. By taking control of their actions and outcomes, they gain more control over their circumstances, leading to increased personal and professional power.

In essence, responsibility and power go hand in hand—responsibility enhances the respect, trust, and effectiveness needed to wield and maintain power.

CHAPTER FIVE

Misuse of Power & Power

The relationship between politics and media is one of both symbiosis and tension, with political figures and organizations often seeking to manipulate media to advance their agendas. Politicians recognize the power of media in shaping public opinion, influencing elections, and setting the national discourse. As such, they strategically use media platforms to craft their public image, promote specific policies, or discredit opponents.

Political manipulation of the media can take various forms, from direct tactics like controlling the flow of information through press releases and speeches to indirect approaches such as leveraging media ownership or fostering relationships with journalists. In the digital age, social media has amplified these strategies, allowing politicians to bypass traditional media filters and speak directly to the public. While this manipulation can be seen as a tool to ensure political survival or to rally support, it can also lead to misinformation, biased reporting, and a distortion of public understanding.

Understanding how politicians manipulate media is crucial to comprehending the broader dynamics of modern democracy, where the lines between truth, opinion, and propaganda can sometimes become dangerously blurred. This manipulation not only shapes political narratives but also impacts how societies engage with and interpret the political world around them.

Misuse of power in politics refers to when political leaders or public officials exploit their authority for personal gain or to benefit certain groups, often at the expense of the public good. This can involve corruption, bribery, cronyism, and authoritarian practices. Some common forms of misuse of power include:

Corruption: Political leaders using their position to obtain personal wealth or privileges, often through illegal means, like bribery or embezzlement.

Authoritarianism: When leaders disregard democratic norms and concentrate power in their own hands, weakening checks and balances and undermining democratic institutions.

Nepotism: Appointing friends or family members to positions of power or awarding them government contracts, regardless of their qualifications.

Censorship and Suppression: When a government restricts the press, silences opposition, or curtails freedom of expression to maintain control and limit criticism.

Political Manipulation: Using power to manipulate the public through misleading information, media control, or political tactics that benefit the ruling party, rather than serving the people.

The misuse of political power undermines trust in institutions, weakens the rule of law, and harms citizens, especially the most vulnerable in society. Effective systems of accountability, transparency, and the rule of law are essential in preventing such misuse.

In recent years, corruption in Indian media has gone way beyond the corruption of individual journalists and specific media organisations from planting information or change the opinion and favours received in cash or kind; or either adopted institutionalized from where newspaper and television channels receive funds for publishing or broadcasting information in favour of particular individuals, corporate entities, representative of political parties and candidates contesting elections that is disguised as 'news'. (Thakurta et. al)

Distinction between News and advertising is blurring as advertisement double up as news that have been paid for or when 'news' is published in favour of a particular politicians by selling editorial spaces? In such situation it is difficult to make distinction between News and fake advertisement. Regarding anyi corruption, the media offers a key rule for information about governmental, administrative and business activities to be disseminated throughout society and thus providing the public with a critical capacity to hold those in power accountable. Power and media refer to theoretical perspective within media studies that examines how a concentrated ownership of media outlet by a small of powerful entities significantly influences the contest produced.

Chomsky's concept of "manufacturing Consent" aligns with this theory, arguing that media often serves the interest of the powerful by shaping public opinion through selective reporting. Curran and Seaton that the media are controlled by a small number of companies driven by profit and power. Media are essentially meant to communicate to the masses on issues of public importance, thereby shaping and churning their opinions towards collective responsibilities in a democratic system of governance. The diverse formats of media available now – newspaper, journal, magazines in the print the electronic media of satellite/Cable TVs and the digital era media of internet, social media network – have widened their reach in fulfilling the larger social objective.

Media Power is generally symbolic and persuasive in the sense that the media primarily have the potential to control to some extent the mind of readers or viewers but not directly their actions. Also, given the presence of other sources of information and because the media usually lack access to the sanction that other – Such as legal or bureaucratic institutions may apply in cases of non compliance, mind control by the media can never be complete psychological and socialogical evidence suggests that despite the persuasion symbolic power of media, the audience will generally retain a minimum of autonomy and independence and engage more or less actively instead of purely passively.

Whistle blower play a critical role by reporting they reasonable believe to waste, fraud and abuse in government operations. Whistle blower have a duty to report wrong doing. The law to protect whistle blower will assist in detecting corruption, ensuring better information flow and paving the way for successful prosecution of corrupt individual through clear and protected processes. The benefits of whistle blower act are helping combat fraud, avoids reputational damage, prevents issues escalating, reduces losses, Raises awareness and create an open culture.

Print and digital media houses in India significantly impact public opinion, political awareness and social change by providing information, shaping opinion and holding authorities accountable with print media playing a foundational role in informing citizens while digital media offers wider reach and faster dissemination of news. Benefits of print media in India are public awareness through newspaper and magazines have historically been crucial for delivering news and information to a large audience, especially in rural areas where internet access may be limited. Print media plays a vital role in shaping public opinion on political issues by providing information in – depth analysis and Commentary.

The impact of print and digital media in India has been transformative across various aspects of society, including communication, education, business, and politics. Here's an overview:

Print Media:

Widespread Reach: Despite the rise of digital media, print media still has a strong presence, especially in rural areas where internet penetration remains low. Newspapers and magazines play an essential role in keeping people informed.

Cultural Influence: Print media has deeply influenced Indian culture by promoting local language content, regional stories, and diverse viewpoints.

Education & Awareness: Print media has been crucial in educating the masses, spreading information about government policies, social causes, health, and more. Newspapers like The Times of India, Hindustan Times, and regional publications have shaped public opinion.

Job Creation: The print industry supports millions of jobs, from journalists and editors to distribution workers and printers.

Challenges: With the rise of digital media, print media faces declining readership and revenue from advertisements. Newspapers have had to adjust by offering digital subscriptions and expanding their online presence.

Digital Media:

Rapid Growth: India has witnessed an explosive growth of digital media with the rise of the internet, smartphones, and social media platforms. The internet user base in India has skyrocketed, reaching over 600 million users.

Democratization of Information: Digital media has provided a platform for diverse voices, enabling individuals from different backgrounds to share opinions, raise awareness, and challenge established narratives. Social media platforms like Facebook, Twitter, YouTube, and Instagram are central to this shift.

Influence on Politics: Digital media has transformed political communication. Political parties now use digital platforms for campaigning, sharing manifestos, and engaging with voters. Social media has played a key role in movements like #MeToo, #InMyName, and even in elections.

Business and Advertising: The shift to digital has dramatically changed business models, with businesses using online platforms for advertising, sales, and customer engagement. Digital ads, search engine marketing, and influencer marketing are now integral parts of India's advertising sector.

Challenges: The rise of misinformation and fake news on digital platforms is a significant concern. There are also privacy issues and digital literacy challenges, especially in rural areas where access to technology may be limited.

Both print and digital media have their own distinct impacts on Indian society. While print media remains an important tool for traditional information dissemination, digital media has brought about faster, more interactive, and widely accessible platforms for communication. The future likely lies in a hybrid model, where both forms of media complement each other.

Investigate journalism in print media can hold authorities accountable by exposing corruption and malpractices. Print publications often reflect and shape cultural trends and societal norms; key benefits of digital media in India are rapid dissemination online news platforms and social media enable near instant access to news and information, facilitating faster public response to events. Digital media can reach a much larger audience across geographical boundaries as compared to print. Digital platforms empower individuals to share their perspective and experiences, contributing to diverse viewpoint. Digital media allows for real time interaction through comments, sharing and discussions fostering public dialogue.

Before people cast their vote for a particular political party, their mindset is often influenced by several factors:

Personal Values and Beliefs: People tend to vote for parties that align with their personal values, such as views on social issues, economic policies, or national security. These beliefs can be shaped by family, upbringing, education, and life experiences.

Party Loyalty: Some individuals vote based on loyalty to a political party, either due to family tradition, long-standing political affiliation, or a sense of identity with the party's history and principles.

Current Events: People's voting choices are often influenced by recent events, including the economy, national crises, or the performance of incumbent leaders. A person's perspective on how well the current government is handling issues will shape their vote.

Candidate Appeal: While the party is important, the individual candidates running for office and their personal characteristics—such as charisma, trustworthiness, and communication skills—play a major role in shaping voter preferences.

Social Influence: Peer pressure, social media, community leaders, and discussions within social networks can significantly impact a person's voting decision. The influence of others, including family and friends, can reinforce or challenge their views.

Media Exposure: The news, advertisements, debates, and campaigns heavily influence how people think about political parties and candidates. The framing of issues in the media can sway opinions, often based on how facts are presented or interpreted.

Perceived Impact: Voters might assess how their vote will affect their personal life and the country's future. This involves considering how a party's policies will impact their economic situation, job prospects, healthcare, education, and social welfare.

Ultimately, voters are influenced by a mix of rational evaluations and emotional reactions, and their final decision often involves a complex interplay of these factors.

Case Study: Media Manipulation and Political Influence in India
Introduction
In India, the relationship between politics and media is both complex and controversial. The political landscape in the country often influences media reporting, and the media is frequently accused of being either too aligned with or too critical of certain political factions. The manipulation of media for political purposes has become a significant concern, especially in the context of India's diverse political environment and rapid media growth. This case study explores the ways in which politics manipulates media in India, illustrating the impact on public opinion, journalism ethics, and democratic processes.

Background
India, as the world's largest democracy, has a thriving media industry. It includes an extensive network of newspapers, television channels, and an ever-expanding digital media presence. The political landscape in India is marked by a large number of regional parties, national parties, and diverse ideologies. Media outlets often align themselves with specific political parties or ideologies, leading to concerns about biased reporting and its influence on public opinion.

Key Examples of Media Manipulation
1. Paid News and Advertorials
Paid news refers to news stories presented as journalistic content but funded by political parties, businesses, or individuals. This often blurs the

line between advertising and journalism.

For example, during the 2009 Indian general elections, reports surfaced about a growing trend of political parties paying media houses to publish positive stories or to downplay their negative aspects. This manipulation leads to biased information reaching the public and distorts the election process.

Advertorials, which are advertisements disguised as editorial content, have also become a tool for politicians. Media outlets often publish political content disguised as regular news pieces, benefiting both the media owners and politicians who seek to influence voters.

2. Selective Reporting and Agenda Setting

Political parties often exert control over media outlets by shaping their coverage to fit their agenda. For example, a ruling party may pressure media outlets to focus on their achievements, while minimizing coverage of scandals or failures.

A prominent example of this selective reporting can be seen in the coverage of the BJP (Bharatiya Janata Party) during its rise in power, where media houses sympathetic to the party often emphasized the party's economic reforms and national security measures while underreporting or downplaying controversies involving its leadership.

Media outlets with clear political affiliations may avoid highlighting certain issues altogether, choosing instead to push forward a party's agenda by framing news in a way that resonates with their political base.

3. Social Media Manipulation

The rise of social media in India has changed the dynamics of media manipulation. Political parties and politicians use social media platforms like Twitter, Facebook, and WhatsApp to directly influence public opinion.

In the 2014 and 2019 general elections, the BJP used social media effectively to spread its political message and counter the opposition. By employing "troll armies" and social media influencers, the party created a narrative that resonated with the electorate.

Social media also serves as a platform for fake news and disinformation campaigns. Political operatives use fake accounts and bots to spread false stories, manipulate narratives, and create divisions among the public. This often involves the distortion of facts, spreading of rumors, or exaggeration of issues to influence voters.

4. Television News and Political Ownership

A significant portion of the Indian television media is owned or controlled by political figures or businesses with political affiliations. For example, some media tycoons with ties to certain political parties often influence content direction.

Channels like Republic TV (owned by Arnab Goswami) have been accused of favoring the BJP. The channel's editorial content, tone, and style of coverage often align with the party's political objectives. Critics argue that the channel uses sensationalism and polarizing rhetoric to shape public opinion.

Similarly, NDTV, seen as pro-Congress in its early years, has faced accusations of aligning with the opposition during periods of Congress rule, and this has been reflected in the way certain news events are covered.

5. Censorship and Pressure on Journalists

Political influence in India extends beyond media outlets to the individual journalists and reporters. Journalists often face threats, harassment, and pressure from political forces to toe the party line.

The case of Gauri Lankesh, an investigative journalist and editor of Lankesh Patrike, illustrates the dangers faced by independent journalists. Lankesh was killed in 2017, allegedly by right-wing extremists, due to her outspoken views on Hindutva and her criticism of political parties in power.

There are numerous instances where journalists or media houses that criticize the government or expose corruption are subjected to legal action, threats, and even violence. This stifles free speech and forces many journalists to practice self-censorship.

Consequences of Media Manipulation

Distortion of Public Opinion

Media manipulation, especially in the context of selective reporting and fake news, distorts public opinion. The public is often fed with biased or incomplete information, which influences their decision-making, especially during elections.

Erosion of Trust in Media

As the media becomes more polarized and aligned with specific political parties, the credibility of journalism suffers. Audiences find it difficult to trust media outlets, as they begin to perceive them as mouthpieces for political interests rather than independent sources of information.

Threat to Democracy

A manipulated media environment undermines the foundations of democracy by limiting the public's access to unbiased information. The role of media as a "watchdog" is compromised, and people are less informed about government policies, corruption, and critical issues, which impedes accountability.

Impact on Elections

The manipulation of media through paid news, biased reporting, and social media manipulation directly influences the outcome of elections. Voters may be misled into supporting candidates or parties based on misinformation, which distorts the democratic process.

The power of media—whether print, digital, or broadcast—is immense and can influence public opinion, shape policy, and affect social change. To use the power of media accurately and effectively, it is crucial to ensure ethical practices, responsibility, and integrity in reporting, as well as promoting engagement with factual and reliable information. Here are some ways to ensure the accurate and effective use of media power:

1. Promote Media Literacy:

Education: Educating the public about how to critically evaluate information is essential. Media literacy empowers audiences to discern between credible and unreliable sources, helping them avoid misinformation or biased content.

Teaching Critical Thinking: Encourage the audience to ask questions, cross-check information, and understand the context in which the news is presented. Critical thinking tools are necessary to challenge misleading or sensationalized narratives.

2. Ensure Objectivity and Balance:

Neutral Reporting: Media outlets should strive for neutrality, providing balanced coverage of events without favoring one side. Journalists and content creators should present multiple viewpoints and avoid sensationalism.

Avoiding Bias: Media professionals must be mindful of inherent biases—whether political, cultural, or social—and ensure their content is not skewed by personal or organizational interests.

3. Fact-Checking and Accuracy:

Verification: Media organizations should prioritize fact-checking and verify the authenticity of information before publication. This can help combat fake news and misinformation.

Accountability: If errors are made, it's important to promptly correct them and issue clarifications. Transparent practices build trust with the audience.

4. Ethical Journalism:

Adherence to Ethical Standards: Journalists must adhere to established ethical guidelines, such as avoiding plagiarism, respecting privacy, and ensuring fairness.

Responsibility to Society: Media has a responsibility to inform and educate the public rather than just entertain. Reporting should be sensitive to the impact it may have on society, especially in areas like politics, health, and social justice.

5. Engagement and Dialogue:

Interactive Platforms: Media, especially digital, should encourage interaction with its audience through comments, discussions, and debates. This two-way communication fosters informed dialogue and broadens the spectrum of viewpoints.

Engagement with Experts: Featuring experts or credible sources in discussions can help provide depth to news stories. Panel discussions, podcasts, and interviews with professionals in relevant fields can offer greater insights.

6. Encourage Accountability and Transparency:

Public Accountability: Media organizations must hold themselves accountable for the content they produce. This includes being transparent about the editorial process, funding sources, and any affiliations that may influence their content.

Addressing Bias and Conflicts of Interest: Being transparent about potential biases (e.g., political affiliations or financial interests) ensures that the audience can critically assess the media's output.

7. Social Media Responsibility:

Combating Misinformation: Social media platforms should take responsibility for curbing the spread of misinformation, particularly during crises or elections. Using fact-checking organizations, AI-driven tools, and user reporting mechanisms can help flag and correct misleading information.

Promote Positive Change: Social media should be used for campaigns that promote social awareness, public health, and civic participation. Positive use of social media can drive social change and encourage collective action.

8. Advocate for Social Good:

Public Service Campaigns: Media can play a crucial role in spreading awareness on critical social issues such as health, environmental protection, and human rights. By providing reliable information, media can empower individuals to make informed decisions and engage in meaningful actions.

Focus on Solutions: Media can help by not just highlighting problems but also offering solutions. Reporting on how communities or individuals are successfully tackling issues can inspire others.

9. Protect Freedom of Press:

Advocacy for Press Freedom: An independent and free press is essential for a vibrant democracy. Supporting the rights of journalists and media outlets to operate without fear of censorship or retaliation is key to ensuring that media can serve the public effectively.

Safeguarding Against Authoritarian Influence: Media should resist manipulation by powerful political or corporate interests, especially when that influence limits the free exchange of ideas and facts.

10. Innovate and Evolve with Technology:

Leverage Technology for Reach: Digital platforms provide powerful tools like podcasts, videos, interactive content, and live broadcasts, all of which can enhance media's reach and impact. Media can leverage these to deliver information in formats that resonate with diverse audiences.

Adapt to New Trends: Media must adapt to new trends like the rise of mobile news consumption, social media influence, and interactive platforms to stay relevant and effective in influencing public opinion.

Case Study: How Politics Manipulate Media

Introduction

In many countries, media serves as a critical source of information, shaping public opinion and influencing political outcomes. However, political actors have often manipulated the media to shape narratives, control information, and enhance their political power. One of the most profound examples of media manipulation in politics can be seen in the relationship between the government and media outlets in authoritarian regimes, as well as in more democratic systems where political influence over media remains significant.

This case study examines the ways in which politics manipulate the media using the example of Vladimir Putin's Russia and the U.S. 2016 Presidential Election, with a focus on the role of media in spreading political influence and misinformation.

Case Study: Influence of Politicians on Media in the USA

Introduction

In the United States, the relationship between politicians and media has always been complex. Politicians use media to reach the public, shape their image, and push forward their policy agendas, while media outlets act as gatekeepers, determining how political narratives are presented. The dynamic between these two entities can lead to a variety of outcomes, from constructive political discourse to attempts at media manipulation. This case study explores how politicians influence media in the USA, analyzing both direct and indirect strategies.

1. Direct Influence: Using Media Platforms for Political Gain

A. Social Media as a Tool for Direct Communication

In recent years, social media platforms have become one of the most powerful tools for politicians to communicate directly with the public. Politicians can bypass traditional media outlets and use platforms like Twitter, Facebook, and Instagram to broadcast their messages, present policies, and sometimes, challenge the media itself.

Example: Donald Trump's use of Twitter

Donald Trump, during his presidency, frequently used Twitter as a direct communication channel. He was able to bypass traditional media filters, setting the agenda for news cycles and even breaking significant news himself.

His tweets would often set the tone of the media coverage for the day, forcing news outlets to respond or report on his statements, sometimes leading to controversy or misinformation. His use of Twitter helped solidify his populist approach, presenting himself as a voice for the "common people" who were "ignored" by mainstream media.

B. Press Conferences and Public Speeches

Politicians also hold regular press conferences or give speeches to directly influence media coverage. These events are often carefully scripted and serve as a controlled environment where politicians present their narratives, policies, and stances on various issues.

Example: Obama's Town Halls

President Barack Obama frequently held town halls and public forums where he directly engaged with the American public through the media. These events were often broadcast live on major TV networks, allowing Obama to articulate his vision for the country and counter any media criticisms in real-time.

The town halls also acted as a way to engage with the public on hot-button issues, like healthcare reform, allowing him to guide media discussions in ways that aligned with his political agenda.

2. Indirect Influence: Shaping Media Narratives

A. Press Releases and Media Coverage

Politicians and their teams frequently send out press releases or make statements to media outlets in an attempt to shape the narrative around an issue. These releases often serve as the basis for media stories, meaning that the initial framing of an issue comes from the politician's perspective.

Example: The Clinton-Lewinsky Scandal

During the Clinton administration, the Monica Lewinsky scandal was covered extensively by the media. However, the way the story was framed was influenced heavily by the statements and spin put out by President Bill Clinton's media team. They attempted to control the narrative, initially denying any wrongdoing, and later trying to shape public perception around the scandal through media responses.

B. Lobbying and Relationship Building with Journalists

Politicians often have close relationships with journalists and media executives. They may exert indirect influence by giving certain journalists exclusive access, granting interviews, or providing "off the record" information to shape future reporting.

Example: Political "Leaks" to the Press

Political figures sometimes leak information to journalists to influence public opinion, weaken rivals, or even manipulate media coverage to their benefit. For example, the Watergate scandal in the 1970s saw leaks from within the Nixon administration that eventually led to the downfall of the president. Journalists like Bob Woodward and Carl Bernstein were instrumental in uncovering the story.

C. Media Ownership and Political Bias

Many media outlets in the USA have close ties with political parties or ideologies, which can influence their coverage. Politicians may engage with media owners to steer the editorial stance of particular outlets in their favor.

Example: Rupert Murdoch's Fox News and Conservative Politics

Rupert Murdoch's ownership of Fox News has often been cited as an example of how media outlets can be aligned with a particular political agenda. Fox News has been criticized for promoting conservative political views and, at times, acting as a mouthpiece for Republican politicians.

Politicians, particularly Republicans, have used Fox News as a platform for their messages, knowing that the network's audience is likely to align with their views. In return, Fox News offers politicians a stage to reach a massive conservative audience, reinforcing political narratives that align with the network's editorial stance.

3. The Role of Media in Political Influence

While politicians influence media, media also plays a key role in shaping political discourse. Politicians may attempt to shape narratives, but they are often at the mercy of how journalists and editors choose to report their messages.

A. Media as a Check on Power

The media also serves as an important check on political power. Investigative journalism often holds politicians accountable, uncovering corruption, scandals, and other forms of misconduct.

Example: Watergate Scandal

Investigative journalists Bob Woodward and Carl Bernstein of The Washington Post exposed the Watergate scandal, which eventually led to the resignation of President Richard Nixon.

This case is one of the clearest examples of how media can act as a counterbalance to political power, and the role of investigative journalists in keeping politicians in check.

B. The "Echo Chamber" Effect

In today's fragmented media landscape, partisan news outlets often create "echo chambers" where audiences are exposed primarily to information that confirms their pre-existing beliefs. Politicians use this dynamic to their advantage by tailoring messages to specific media outlets or even by creating their own platforms.

Example: The 2020 Election and Disinformation Campaigns

During the 2020 presidential election, there were numerous disinformation campaigns across various social media platforms, often fueled by political actors or their allies. These campaigns aimed to sway public opinion by targeting specific groups with misleading or false information.

The role of both social media and traditional news outlets in spreading and amplifying these messages highlights the intersection of media and political influence in shaping public perception and behavior.

The relationship between politicians and media in the USA is a dynamic one, characterized by both direct and indirect influences. Politicians use media platforms to communicate with the public, shape narratives, and promote their political agendas, while media outlets both serve as a platform for and a check on political power. The increasing prominence of social media has further transformed this relationship, allowing politicians more direct control over their messages, but also creating new challenges in terms of misinformation and media manipulation. Ultimately, both politicians and media share a mutual dependency, and their interactions continue to evolve with the changing landscape of modern media.

1. Vladimir Putin's Russia: Control of Media for Political Gain

Overview of the Media Landscape

In Russia, the government has exerted extensive control over media outlets, particularly television, which remains the most influential medium in the country. Under Putin's leadership, the Kremlin has implemented strategies that effectively centralize media power under the state. By 2015, the majority of major Russian television channels were owned or heavily influenced by the government, with only a few independent outlets left, often working in a constrained environment.

Methods of Manipulation

State-Controlled Television: Putin's government has used state-controlled television to promote its policies and suppress dissenting views. State channels, such as Russia 1 and Channel One, focus on promoting the government's agenda, while suppressing stories that could harm Putin's image or criticize the Kremlin.

Censorship and Suppression of Dissent: Political dissent is often suppressed through media censorship. Independent journalists and media outlets that criticize the government face persecution, including harassment, closure, and legal action. Media outlets critical of the government have been silenced, with some media executives being arrested or killed.

Creation of a Positive Image of the Leader: The Russian media has become a powerful tool in shaping the public perception of Putin as a strong, decisive leader. His image is carefully crafted through propaganda and selective coverage

A network error occurred. Please check your connection and try again. If this issue persists please contact us through our help center at help.openai.com.

Conclusion

The manipulation of media by political forces in India is a concerning trend that affects the media's role as the fourth estate. Whether through paid news, selective reporting, social media manipulation, or direct pressure on journalists, political actors are increasingly influencing how information is disseminated to the public. The consequences of such practices are far-reaching, including a loss of trust in the media, distortion of public opinion, and undermining the democratic process. In such a complex media landscape, it is crucial for both the public and media organizations to strive for transparency, ethical journalism, and accountability. Both print and digital media have their own distinct impacts on Indian society. While print media remains an important tool for traditional information dissemination, digital media has brought about faster, more interactive, and widely accessible platforms for communication. The future likely lies in a hybrid model, where both forms of media complement each other.

In conclusion, the relationship between media and power is complex and multifaceted. Media has the ability to shape public perception, influence opinions, and control the flow of information, which in turn gives it substantial power in society. This power can be used for both positive and negative ends, depending on who controls the media and how it is utilized. On one hand, media can be a tool for social change, awareness, and empowerment, providing a platform for marginalized voices and promoting democracy. On the other hand, it can also be used to manipulate public opinion, perpetuate misinformation, or serve the interests of powerful elites. The dynamics of media and power continue to evolve with technological advancements and the rise of digital platforms, making it more important than ever to critically assess how media shapes our world.

IDEOLOGY AND POWER

CHAPTER SEVEN

SELF ACTUALIZATION AND POWER

Self-actualization and power are two critical concepts that intersect in both personal and societal contexts, particularly in the realm of politics and leadership.

Self-actualization is the process of realizing and fulfilling one's potential, often considered the highest level of psychological development. This concept was introduced by psychologist Kurt Goldstein and later popularized by Abraham Maslow as part of his hierarchy of needs. According to Maslow, self-actualization is the pinnacle of human motivation, achieved once basic needs such as physiological needs, safety, love, and esteem are met.

Self-actualization involves personal growth, self-awareness, creativity, and the pursuit of one's true passions. It is the state of being where an individual feels fully aligned with their authentic self, displaying qualities such as independence, resilience, and a sense of purpose. It is unique to each person, as it is shaped by their values, talents, and experiences.

Maslow believed that self-actualized individuals are more likely to engage in meaningful and fulfilling activities, be at peace with themselves, and demonstrate traits like empathy, problem-solving ability, and spontaneity. However, it's not a fixed state but rather a continual process of growth and self-discovery.

Self-Actualization refers to the process of realizing one's full potential and striving to become the best version of oneself. It is often associated with personal growth, fulfillment, and the pursuit of meaning. This concept was popularized by psychologist Abraham Maslow as the pinnacle of his hierarchy of needs, emphasizing the realization of personal talents, creativity, and a deeper connection to one's purpose. In the political realm, self-actualization could involve leaders who not only seek to grow personally but also work towards the betterment of society, guided by a vision of authenticity, ethics, and meaningful contribution.

Power, on the other hand, is the capacity to influence, control, or direct the behavior of individuals or groups. It can manifest in different forms, such as coercive power, legitimate power, expert power, or referent power. In the political context, power is central to decision-making, governance, and the ability to affect change. While power is often associated with authority and control, it can also be a means to enact positive transformation when used responsibly.

The intersection of self-actualization and power raises important questions: How do individuals in positions of power navigate their personal growth while influencing others? Can one truly realize their potential while holding substantial power, or does power corrupt the process of self-actualization? This dynamic plays a crucial role in shaping the motivations and actions of political leaders, and ultimately, it influences the course of societies and their governance structures.

Political Gridlock and Compromise: Political polarization and division within government can result in gridlock, where little progress is made on important policy issues. In such environments, public policy may either stagnate or become a series of compromises that may not fully address the needs of society.

Overall, the political landscape heavily influences public policy, as decisions are made based on political considerations, values, and agendas. These political dynamics shape the policies that affect people's daily lives, from healthcare to education to economic opportunities.

Abraham Maslow's Hierarchy of Needs is a psychological theory that suggests human beings are motivated by a series of hierarchical needs. These needs must be met in a specific order, from the most basic to the most complex. The hierarchy is usually depicted as a pyramid with five levels:

Physiological Needs: These are the basic biological requirements for survival, such as food, water, shelter, sleep, and warmth.

Safety Needs: Once physiological needs are met, individuals seek safety and security, including physical safety, financial security, health, and protection from harm.

Love and Belongingness Needs: This level involves the desire for social connections, relationships, love, affection, and belonging to a group, such as family, friends, or a community.

Esteem Needs: These involve the desire for self-esteem, respect from others, recognition, achievement, and a sense of accomplishment.

Self-Actualization: The highest level of the hierarchy, self-actualization represents the realization of one's potential, creativity, and personal growth. It's about becoming the best version of oneself and pursuing individual passions and goals.

Maslow believed that lower-level needs must be satisfied before higher-level needs can be pursued. This theory has had a significant influence on psychology, education, and personal development.

Self-actualization and ultimate power in politics are two complex concepts that often intersect, especially when individuals in political spheres seek both personal growth and influence. Here's how they might relate:

Self-Actualization in Politics:

Definition: Self-actualization refers to realizing and fulfilling one's potential and capabilities. In a political context, it involves a politician or leader striving for personal growth, ethical behavior, and a sense of purpose in their work.

Example: A leader might view their political position as a platform not only to gain power but also to make a genuine impact on society, addressing fundamental issues like social justice, equality, or the environment. Their goal isn't just to attain power but to embody their ideals and help others achieve their potential as well.

Impact on Leadership: Politicians who are self-actualized often inspire others by acting with authenticity and a clear vision. They work not just for the maintenance of power but for the betterment of society and their personal moral development.

Ultimate Power in Politics:

Definition: Ultimate power refers to the supreme control and influence over political, economic, and social systems. It can manifest in various forms, from authoritarian control to widespread democratic influence.

Types of Power: There are different forms of political power:

Coercive power: Relying on force or threats.

Legitimate power: Based on position or authority within a political system.

Expert power: Derived from specialized knowledge or skills.

Referent power: Based on the personal appeal or charisma of the leader.

Example: Leaders like dictators often pursue ultimate power through coercion and control. On the other hand, democratic leaders may attain significant influence through persuasive policies, charisma, and public trust.

Interplay Between Self-Actualization and Ultimate Power:

Conflict: The pursuit of ultimate power can sometimes contradict self-actualization. A political leader who seeks power for the sake of self-aggrandizement or control might lose sight of personal growth or the well-being of others. In such cases, power can become a tool for personal insecurity or fear rather than self-fulfillment.

Synergy: In some cases, political leaders might seek power not just for self-interest but to create a lasting, positive impact. Here, their pursuit of ultimate power is intertwined with their personal growth and a desire to see society thrive. Their actions become a reflection of self-actualization because they align with their deepest values and a sense of responsibility.

For example, Nelson Mandela combined elements of personal growth (self-actualization) with the quest for power to dismantle apartheid and transform South Africa. His leadership was rooted in his personal experiences of growth, and his power was used in service of a greater purpose.

Link between Maslow's Hierarchy and Power in Politics:

Physiological and Safety Needs:

Power Source: Political leaders or parties often address these basic needs in times of crisis, such as natural disasters or economic instability. They offer solutions like food security, healthcare, or job creation.

Power in Action: Governments may consolidate power to ensure order and stability, using emergency laws or policies.

Love and Belonging Needs:

Power Source: Politicians often use social groups, such as unions, ethnic groups, or communities, to build support. They tap into identity politics and appeal to a sense of collective belonging.

Power in Action: Political campaigns might focus on unity, creating a sense of solidarity and loyalty among voters.

Esteem Needs:

Power Source: Political leaders try to inspire admiration and respect from their constituents. They may promise recognition, awards, or even symbolic leadership roles.

Power in Action: Political figures may use symbols of status, like national awards, titles, or prestigious positions, to solidify their authority and garner support.

Self-Actualization:

Power Source: Political power can be used to enact policies that promote innovation, creativity, and societal progress. Leaders can also position themselves as agents of change and visionaries.

Power in Action: Rhetoric and policies about self-improvement, education, and advancing human potential are often employed by leaders to appeal to this level of need.

Conclusion:

In political systems, power is often linked to addressing various layers of human needs. Political leaders, by understanding the hierarchy of needs, can influence and motivate citizens by addressing these needs through policy, rhetoric, and action. Politics, thus, revolves around securing power by appealing to the needs that Maslow identified.

In summary, self-actualization in politics focuses on the leader's growth and ethical considerations, while ultimate power focuses on the ability to control and influence. These concepts can coexist harmoniously if a political figure seeks power for constructive purposes aligned with personal values, or they can conflict if power is sought at the expense of integrity or humanity.

Conclusion:

Self-actualization and power are deeply connected concepts, but their relationship is complex. Self-actualization, as defined by Maslow, is the realization of one's fullest potential and the pursuit of personal growth, authenticity, and fulfillment. It involves a deep understanding of oneself, mastery of one's abilities, and contributing to society in a meaningful way.

Power, on the other hand, often refers to the ability to influence or control others and resources. While power can be seen as a means to assert control or achieve external goals, self-actualization is about inner growth, self-determination, and alignment with one's true purpose.

The intersection of self-actualization and power lies in how power is used. When a person is self-actualized, they are more likely to use their power responsibly, with empathy, and for the benefit of others, rather than for domination or control. In contrast, those who are not self-actualized may seek power for validation or status, often at the expense of others.

In conclusion, true power is most effective and meaningful when it aligns with self-actualization. People who are self-actualized possess the inner strength to wield power in ways that support their growth and contribute to the well-being of others, fostering positive change and creating a more compassionate society.